# GOSPEL FAMILY

## A Guide to the Kingdom

ROB AND GAIA CARVELL

# Dedication

*We would like to dedicate this book to our Heavenly Father and to the coming Kingdom of Heaven where all humankind can have the opportunity to experience true love and true happiness.*

*It is through the total sacrifice and love of our lord Jesus Christ and Sun Myung Moon, His second coming that we are blessed to be able to share in this, and through the faithfulness and filial piety of his son and heir Hyung Jin Moon that this work continues today.*

# Table of Contents

# Preface

I grew up many years ago in what I understood to be a "normal" household. I had a loving mother and father, a brother and a sister. We had cousins, aunts and uncles around as well as a couple of grandparents. I never met anyone in my childhood who was from a single parent family, but I had heard about them as people who we should feel sorry for because it was probably due to some serious accident. Attending the local church was our regular Sunday schedule and Sunday lunch was the time for the family to sit, eat, relax and chat. This was how normal society worked after all.

Fast forward fifty years and look around, and we can see that the family has come under increasingly serious attack. There are many sides of this – the media promoting free sex and confused relations; the public school system pushing a socialist doctrine instead of good education; moral and ethical decline and the sidelining of religious values. Add to this, government programs designed to encourage single parent families through a combination of selective taxation and financial handouts. In fact we see Christianity taken out of schools and even being turned into a source of bigotry and cause of our nation's ills in many movies, TV shows and other forms of "entertainment".

Our desire is not to return to the "good ol' days", but to progress to great new days after this failed experiment in social engineering that we have lived through. In this book we would like to discuss the *true value and purpose of the family* from a biblical and God centered perspective.

Historically the family has been the building block of society, and just as the family goes, so does the society. In early America, Christianity, in many forms, was the foundation of the family. Different forms of Christianity had arrived on America's shores from Europe and religious freedom based on Christian ethics was one of the pillars of the founding of this country. It was this Judeo Christian way of life that helped America to become the greatest country in the world. Taking out a foundational pillar results in the collapse of a building and will also do the same for society.

We will be looking at practical ways to rebuild and strengthen the family and in so doing, rebuild and strengthen society. The basis we have chosen for this first book in the Gospel Family series is the Family Pledge given to us by Rev Sun Myung Moon, the Lord of the Second Advent. We will look at and discuss each pledge in order and find the incredible inspiration and direction that is there.

My wife Gaia had the strong inspiration to write this book a while back, and she turned to me to actively put words to paper. I have been strongly blessed by so doing as I have received so much education and guidance from God in the process. The bulk of the teaching is directly from Rev Moon's own explanations plus added insights from his heir and successor, Hyung Jin Moon. Gaia felt that I was being a little to "vertical" in my discussion and so added a loving Mother's touch at the end of each chapter under the heading "Gaia's Gems".

We sincerely hope that you can receive the same God's love and inspirational guidance from reading this book as we did in writing it. Please join us in building His kingdom on the earth!

With Christ's love. Thank you.

# Introduction

The contents of this book are based on the Family Pledge, given to us by Rev Sun Myung Moon, the Lord of the Second Advent.

There are 8 pledges in all, each one of them building on the previous one.

The expression Family Pledge never existed until now. Rev Moon, following the way of Jesus Christ, went through a course of tremendous suffering, paying the price to bring victory for God. On that foundation, one of the blessings he gave us is the Family Pledge. It shows us a path to establish the Kingdom of Heaven. If you carefully study the Family Pledge, you can see that its contents explain that total liberation will be granted based on going through these steps. Those who have absolute faith, love and obedience do not belong in the family realm of the fallen world but in the family realm of the Kingdom of Heaven. This true family can be established based on true love. Mind and body that were separated because of false love can now be united and eventually all of God's children can be united in peace, love and harmony.

In this book you will see the term "Fall" many times. This is referring to the story in Genesis 3 that explains how Adam and Eve fell away from God and were banished form the Garden of Eden. We look upon this as the misuse of love, a sexual act and therefore causing the human lineage to no longer belong to God but to Satan. Jesus said in John 8:44-45 *"You are of your father the devil, and the lusts of your father you will do. He was a murderer from the beginning, and abode not in the truth, because there is no truth in him. When he speaks a lie, he speaks of his own: for he is a liar, and the father of it."*

Until now, Christians have thought that only Adam and Eve fell. They did not realize that Adam's *family* fell. Adam and Eve's children also fell when Cain killed Abel. This allowed Satan to dominate humankind as their false father. If Abel had won over Cain through true love, restoration could have happened right there and then on the family level and this miserable history of suffering would not have happened. One of the key actions that happened in the bible in the course of God's constant efforts to restore His children is this victory of Abel over Cain. The first such victory is the story in Genesis chapters 25 through 36 with the culmination in chapter 33. Jacob and Esau were the twin sons of Isaac, Esau being the eldest representing Cain. Eventually Jacob, representing Abel, won the heart of his elder brother, thereby preventing Esau from killing him.

An understanding of these two actions – the Fall and the victory of Abel and Cain – will help you to understand the actions associated with the family pledge.
The third essential is the "Blessing". We use this term to describe the Marriage of the Lamb when Christ, at His second coming, takes a bride and restores fallen Eve, bringing into reality the restored Adam and Eve as the "True Parents" of mankind. The True Parents then pass this Blessing of marriage onto all of humankind engrafting

them into the lineage of God. Hence all the mass weddings that Rev Moon has officiated over.

I have just taken 4 paragraphs to very briefly explain The Divine Principle (the official teaching of Rev Moon based on his deep prayer and study of the bible) that goes into great detail of Gods constant and 100% effort to restore His children and His ideal. More details will be covered in future books, but I hope that this will help you to understand the immensity of what you are about to read.

# Chapter One

## Commit yourself and family to God and His Kingdom.

**Our family pledges to build the Kingdom of God on earth and in heaven, the original ideal of creation, by centering on true love.**

*And God said, Let us make man in "our" image, after "our" likeness (Gen 1:26)* Who is "our"??

*And God blessed them, and God said unto them, be fruitful, and multiply, and replenish the earth, and subdue it: and have dominion over the fish of the sea, and over the fowl of the air, and over every living thing that moves upon the earth. (Gen 1:28)*

*But seek ye first the kingdom of God, and his righteousness; and all these things shall be added unto you. (Matt 6:33)*

## *Kingdom of God: What is it?*

In the very beginning of the bible we read how God made the creation. Whether we consider this literal or not is unimportant for this discussion. What matters is that God had a purpose. He made the creation as a foundation for his children. Man and women were the final part of the creation, were made in his image (Gen 1:26), and were created to become the lords of creation (Gen 1:28). In other words we are supposed to become fruitful (mature, ready to bear good fruit as beings of true love); multiply and fill the earth; and take dominion over all the creation.

Simply put, this is the Kingdom of God – a place where men and women are mature, loving, free, and responsible. The family is where this starts.

## *The family of True Love*

In creation we see that the higher the created being, the greater the tendency to form lifelong pairs for the sake of procreation.

When we get to the highest created being of all (mankind – God's children made in his image) we see that true love is the critical aspect that brings men and women together.
Love is the true foundation for commitment. The man and the women pledge themselves to each other for better or for worse and ideally do so centered on God. This is the foundation of the family.

The family needs to make a commitment to a life of true love.

A life of true love is not partial or half way. It reaches for the highest ideals, for ourselves and our children and children's children.

With mature, loving, free and responsible individuals (the parents) as the foundation of the family we believe that God, the family and the world can be harmonized. Our responsibilities to serve God, the world and our families completely and simultaneously can be fulfilled through true love. This can happen in a very natural way as we go about our day to day activities in our home and communities.

Before we begin anything in life, we should clarify our purpose. Is not love true or false according to the purposes lying deep in our hearts? A prerequisite to living with true love and becoming a true family is to orient ourselves to a purpose that is true. Once our aim is true, then everything we do contributes to our ultimate success.

Jesus himself came preaching the Kingdom of God. (Mark 1:15) He taught his followers, "Seek first his kingdom and his righteousness" (Matt. 6:33), and promised God's abundant prosperity and happiness in return. Likewise, we commit ourselves and our families to becoming partners with Christ in establishing God's Kingdom.

If our family is a true family, devoted to building God's Kingdom, we should live by true love. True love should shine through all our family relationships: among husband and wife, parents and children, brothers and sisters. In this way, we set a good example at home. Furthermore, a true family gives generous service to the community. We should shed the light of goodness and love upon our neighbors and relatives, stimulating their hearts to multiply charity, peace and good will.

Jesus said: You are the light of the world. A city set on a hill cannot be hid. Nor do men light a lamp and put it under a bushel, but on a stand, and it gives light to all in the house. Let your light so shine before men, that they may see your good works and give glory to your Father who is in heaven. – (Matt. 5:14-16)

## *What is a "family"?*

The family is not just parents and children, but includes the entire family environment.

A family is multi-generational vertically and multi-cellular horizontally: grandparents, parents, children, grandchildren, etc.; and aunts, uncle, cousins, etc.

They are a family through the abiding presence of true love. This true love is both spiritual and physical. Spiritually, true love means that each family member lives for the sake of the whole family.

Physically, true love means that all family members are biologically connected in one blood lineage.

The home is part of the family. It presents the face of the family to the world. Every home you go to uniquely expresses the nature of the family living there.

The family includes its rightful possessions of goods and land. Land historically has been a means of providing for the family.

We also care for the things of creation as a type of family members. Farmers often have communication with their animals, and house pets are definitely considered part of the family these days. Garden plants are also objects of love and care and respond accordingly. Various scientific studies have shown how plants respond to love.

The family also extends vertically through the generations. If we were spiritually open, we could sense that our ancestors often visit us. Seven generations of ancestors influence our family life, according to the Bible. We should respect our ancestors and be grateful for what they bequeathed to us.

In traditional oriental society the "household gods" had a special altar. They protected the home. These often were angels. Angels visited Abraham and Sarah, and he showed them great hospitality. These angels protected Lot and his family in the city of Sodom.

God can dwell in our family if we invite Him. Our Heavenly Father is ever supporting and protecting us and wants to live life with us and through us.

We have to beware though, as evil spirits may also come in. We should be sensitive to the spiritual presences in our home, especially to protect the children. Praying, reading God's words and living for others as a family creates the good spiritual atmosphere in which God and good spirits can dwell. — & wards off evil dwellers.

Thus, the family is a community of heaven and spirit, humanity and creation. These three dimensions are intertwined in our lives and there should be harmony among them through true love. The Chinese character for "blessing" means the harmony of God, humankind, and the earth within the will of God.

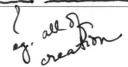
eg. all of creation

Unfortunately, although this was our Heavenly Father's original ideal, things did not work out this way. Lucifer tempted Eve, Eve tempted Adam and the fall took place. God kicked mankind out of the Garden of Eden (Gen 3:23-24) and the land was cursed (Gen 3:17-18). Adam's family now had to go the way of suffering and this can be seen in our human history of violence and selfishness.

Our motivation in publishing this book is to revive and strengthen the original ideals and move us towards the kingdom of Heaven on earth. We know that there are many good people and families in the world but we can see so much evil in society. We need true love families to increase in number and strength to take dominion over society by setting the standard by which it operates.

In order to accomplish this and return the family to God we have a few actions that can reverse the process that created this evil society. These actions are the reverse of what happened at the fall.

1. See things from God's point of view. Have the attitude of true love – live for the sake of others as individuals and a family.
2. Keep your proper position. The children should honor and respect their elders and in that way learn from them. Through this they learn the vertical connection to God
3. Maintain proper dominion by putting God first in our hearts and actions.
4. Multiply good. Love and care for others around you as both individuals and a family. Pay it forward.

In this way the family as a whole acts to give true love. Children are safe, loved and happy and grow into mature and responsible adults.

Grandparents are loved, respected and taken care of in their old age and experience the joy of seeing their progeny blossom.

Great leaders appear with mature and responsible attitudes of service to those they lead. *If they come from a good family*

And society can become a caring and safe place to live. Individuals and families can coexist peacefully as all share a common bond of connection to God because God is the origin of true love.

## *The Four Position foundation.*

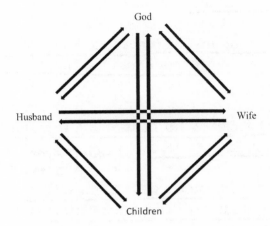

In the teachings of Rev. Sun Myung Moon the basis for the above relationship is the Four Position Foundation.
This means there are four positions, with God, parents and children all playing a critical role.

This is the foundation for the proper functioning of the family. These four positions in good give and take are the model or pattern for the family. *Give and take* means that you both give and receive in a relationship.

This four position foundation has both vertical and horizontal dimensions.

The "vertical" dimension refers to the connection to God and is the spiritual or internal aspect. It is invisible to the physical senses.

The "horizontal" dimension refers to the physical aspect of human relations, and is visible and tangible. We call this being centered on God or centered on true love. "Centered on" refers to the motivation of our actions and is the purpose we have in either our vertical internal aspect or our resultant physical relationships.

### *True Love: What is it?*

Before considering the full meaning of a family centered on true love, we should discuss the meaning of "true love".

We see that true love is:
Spontaneous and irrepressible.
Based upon the irresistible desire of the heart.
It is total investment.
Both giving and receiving are unselfish.
Love is freely given and not demanded.
Love can never force itself, but always waits for the response of the beloved. (1 Cor. 13)
Love and freedom exist together or not at all.
Love is the root motivation. It cannot be employed in the service of other motives. This means true love is pure, unadulterated by other motives. Therefore, first love, virginal love, is the strongest. We all desire eternal love, because purity is eternal.

After experiencing betrayal, we tend to hold back, unable to be completely free to give. Only total repentance and confession to the other can overcome the horrible prison that is created in a relationship when one partner violates love. Unfortunately such honesty and repentance rarely happens; divorce is far more likely because of the desire to hide our transgressions.

Love finds and follows the shortest route. It jumps instantaneously from person to person, faster than the speed of light. Love flows through the relationship of two entities, like the circuit created by plus and minus electricity. When there is no connection, love cannot flow.

And just like the two connections that are required for the electricity to flow, a partner is required for love to be fulfilled. No one can make love by himself or herself. Therefore we are unfulfilled and unhappy when we are alone. We are all looking for a partner to whom we can express our love. When someone receives our love and responds with happiness, then we are most happy.

There are different levels on which this can happen.

We can love the creation and it returns beauty to us as a form of love.
Many of us love our pets, because our pets respond to our love more reliably than people do.

But the greatest partners for our love are the members of our own family: Our parents, brothers and sisters, spouse, and children. These partners are provided to us by God through the natural course of life. They are lifetime partners upon whom we can always rely, and in whom we want to invest ourselves.

This is because we are created in the image of God (Gen 1:26). Just as we need an object of love in our lives to bring joy, Heavenly Father Himself needs a partner of love in order for Him to experience joy. For this He invested

Himself totally in the creation. His love is the root and model of true love.

God's love is unconditional. God invested Himself completely in the creation. Even after the objects of His love betrayed Him in the Garden of Eden he kept giving and attempting to find ways to bring mankind back to the Kingdom. Give, forget what you have given, and give again, is the way of true love, and we see Jesus exemplifying this in His life and on the cross.

Without a relationship with the living God, this kind of unconditional love is impossible. If Adam and Eve had remained faithful to Heavenly Father, unconditional love would have been the norm. But because of the fall, selfishness was created. So for us to get back to true unconditional love we need to re-connect to the origin – God, through the One sent by Him, and through that power and grace, overcome selfishness.

Love was the motive and purpose for God's creation of the universe and humankind. Therefore God's love is the source, model and goal of true love. Heavenly Father designed the universe so that love would be the most precious thing and it is the source of life, joy and happiness, even for God.

God created love to be the strongest force. The glue that holds everything together. Heavenly Father created us through the love of our parents and we are supposed to grow to become the dwelling place of God, exemplified by our love for our parents, spouse, children, everyone and everything around us. The Kingdom of heaven is God's original design where true love combined with freedom and responsibility abound.

A true love relationship is (my) responsibility, not the other person's. I am the one to overcome my selfish viewpoint and give unconditionally. If there are problems, I should first look to myself, is my love pure? Do I unconditionally love my spouse? Or do I just expect my spouse to love me?

One of the ways in which selfishness dominates us is the reversal of dominion between the mind and body. The mind, centered on God, is supposed to dominate the body. But in fallen man the body can dominate the mind so completely that we do not follow our conscience. False, self-centered bodily love pushes us to use others to satisfy our self, and forcefully plant our seed where it does not belong. This is the root cause of all evil in the world. This is not true love but true evil!

To practice true love, and overcome the temptation to false love, we can use two methods:

Study and embody God's words, which strengthens the power of the mind.

Discipline the body, making it do what it does not like to do (fasting, prayer vigils, self-sacrifice).

These two methods are contained in the basic teachings of all religions. By subjugating the body, the conscience is liberated, allowing us to fly in the ecstasy of love that is one with God. Take care of your body for the sake of serving others.

## *True love can embrace all people*

As discussed before, we are created in God's image. If we study the bible from the perspective of God's actions, we can get a good idea of what our actions should be. The first thing that jumps out is God's love is not fickle, or here one day and gone the next. He continues to love even when the object of his love messes up. He is always ready to forgive and welcome us back. He also sees what is in our heart and does not judge superficially.

Saul was persecuting and imprisoning Christians but Jesus called and loved him (Acts 9 1:22) to the point where he became one of the greatest disciples (Paul).

In Genesis we read the story of Jacob and Esau (Gen 32 & 33). Here Jacob unconditionally gives of his wealth to his brother Esau who wished to kill him. Esau was so moved by Jacob's love that all thoughts of killing him vanished. Sacrificial love for the enemy is the only way to end hatred, resentment, alienation and violence. Sacrificial love induces the voluntary surrender of the enemy.

## *The proper order of love*

Jesus taught that we should love our neighbor, whom we can see, before claiming that we love God, whom we cannot see, and in the Parable of the Good Samaritan, that everyone in the world is our neighbor. (Luke 10 29:37)

Our life growing up in the family is our training ground teaching us to love, first within the family and then outwards to our neighbor. We learn as an individual to love and live for our family and as a family to love and live for our society.

This continues on by extension as the society living for the nation, the nation living for the world, the world living for the cosmos and the cosmos living for God.

God totally lives for us and so we have a wonderful circular motion of true love flowing through everything.

This means that each member of the family represents the love within the family out into the larger society, and from there throughout the creation in an ever expanding radius. It is in the larger society that that love attains its greatest value: in bringing joy and blessings to others. From the give and take of true love of husband and wife comes true life to the world and the Kingdom of Heaven on earth is created.

We mentioned earlier that "centered on" refers to the motivation of our actions and is the purpose we have in either our vertical internal aspect or our resultant physical relationships.

The family "centered on true love" means that our family's motivation and purpose of existence is true love leading us to live according to the way of true love. → purity of ♥

The way of true love is to live for others in the ever expanding radius. We live for others, serve others, and care for others ahead of ourselves and we seek the goal of true love – the Kingdom of Heaven on earth.

True families centered on true love are the cornerstone of the Kingdom, of God naturally giving of ourselves for the welfare of the wider world. Through commitment to work within our family for the benefit of our local community, we set the standard that can then expand outwards.

By taking responsibility before God, for not only ourselves and family, but on an ever expanding level, we eradicate the need for large suppressive government. Large suppressive government is a reversal of dominion and is basically a cop-out and excuse for not practicing true love. In this period of Kingdom building, true love families are unfortunately a small minority. However, we represent Heavenly Father and His true love. We are an example for others to follow. Isaiah called us to be "a light to the nations" Jesus spoke about letting your light shining forth before men, so that they might glorify God (Matt: 5:16). The Puritans were called to create a "city on a hill," a Christian commonwealth for all the world to see.

We are called, to commit ourselves and family to God and His Kingdom by taking on a responsibility to serve others around us. When we do this, it naturally draws people to us. This makes our family a "central family."

A president is a central family of his nation, a governor of his state, a mayor of his city and a pastor of his church. There are many ways for us to serve in a true love fashion.

As an individual, when one takes a public position, others in the family also become public. A politician campaigns with his wife and children. A spouse and children who support a public person may have to make many sacrifices, they do it and thereby participate in his public mission. They have to take the attitude that "my time is for others. Whatever the needs of my community, I will put them first, even when it impinges on my privacy". It is not about having power.

A central family that protects, nourishes and cares for others, becomes the natural leader in the community.

## *Summary*

Families want to create the Kingdom of God on earth as it is in heaven - the original ideal of creation. This can be done by centering on true love:
Love God.
Love Christ.
Love your neighbor as yourself.
Live for the sake of others.
Take responsibility.
Maintain freedom from repression.
The building of God's Kingdom is not a mysterious supernatural thing floating in from the sky, but a series of actions that we can all do.

## Gaia's Gems for Personal Expansion

## Gaia's Gem 1 - living with INTEGRITY.

Making my spiritual growth as a priority in order to recreate myself with authentic power.
Renew my Commitment.
I commit to know all of myself completely, letting go of any defensive postures, wanting to learn from every interaction focusing on what I can learn about myself.
I have spent most of my life feeding my habit of self-criticism and then projecting the blame of that in my relationships! **Self-acceptance or self-love is a genuine feeling of unconditional loving acceptance of all aspect of myself**. Becoming aware of my emotions, letting myself know all of my feelings and be welcomed into the wholeness of myself as my Heavenly Father does, because I am a sparkle of Him.
Praise Him and commit myself.
Commit to discover who I am from inside-out living from essence.
*"If there is a light in the soul, there will be beauty in a person.*
*If there is beauty in a person, there will be harmony in the* house. family
*If there is harmony in the* house, family *there will be order in the nation.*
*If there is order in the nation, there will be peace in the world "* Who said this?

# Chapter Two

## Commit yourself and family to be filial to God and His Kingdom.

*obedient + respectful of elders, up. God.*

Our family pledges to perfect the dutiful family way of filial sons and daughters in our family, patriots in our nation, saints in the world, and divine sons and daughters in heaven and earth, by centering on true love.

*"You should become sons of filial piety, daughters-in-law of filial piety, then saints of filial piety. Next, you have to become sons of filial piety on the family level before God, centering on purity, pure lineage, and pure love. Your whole family must become children of filial piety, not just you as individuals. Then become families of patriots who are filial, families of saints who are filial, and families of divine sons and daughters who are filial. From that position, you should become representatives of the owner, representatives who are fully capable of becoming princes and princesses who can inherit the kingship of heaven from the individual level up to the level of the cosmos. You should always train yourselves that way. That is what is meant by an owner of The Kingdom. "(SMM)*

In this 2nd chapter of Gospel Family we will look at the Family commitment.

Here we see that we are promising to live a vertically connected life.

As individuals and as children in the family we learn to live for the greater whole. In the previous chapter we learned about the family being the school of true love. When we are loved by our parents we love and respect them in return. Love begets love.

*respect to love → obedience*

Our parents gave us life and as we grow, they continue to love and care for us. We quite naturally respond to this with filial piety. It is not a duty but a natural reaction, a part of growing up in the gospel family.

This is, of course, very idealistic thinking. However, if our original human ancestors had not created selfish individualism by listening to Lucifer in the Garden of Eden, it would have been the normal way of life. It is therefore our goal to restore this.

It is necessary for parents to set the example of true love by loving and caring for the children. This includes tough love guiding their children firmly when required. Children can sense the heart behind a reprimand or punishment and only when it is done motivated by love does it have any real effect. Punishment out of anger, frustration or from a power struggle leads to distrust, alienation and resentment.

Parents will also value and care for the grandparents. In this way we will have 3 or even 4 generational family units at the center of any community and it becomes unnecessary to hand our children or grandparents over to the government or other institutions to be cared for. Parents and grandparents can take care of the children, and parents and children can take care of the grandparents. This is a solid foundation to build society on.

Parents also set the example by serving and sacrificing for the greater whole. If we see our father, in the volunteer fire brigade for example, running to help another family whose house is on fire, we learn that attitude quite naturally.

Unfortunately we are not living in an age of perfection and parents are not perfect. It was for this reason that God made honoring your father and mother an important directive in the 10 commandments: Exodus 20:12 *Honor thy father and thy mother: that thy days may be long upon the land which the LORD thy God giveth thee.*

And which Jesus quoted when asked how to gain eternal life: Matt 19:19 *Honor thy father and thy mother*

As part of restoration history, children need to respect and honor their parents even when they could easily judge them. This paves the way for restoration to take place in the family and fallen nature to be overcome.

In the Bible, we can compare Ham and Isaac in terms of filial piety. Ham disrespected his father Noah, even after Noah's work saved the family from the flood (Gen. 9:2-25) On the other hand, Isaac obeyed his father Abraham, even when Abraham placed him on the altar to be sacrificed (Gen. 15:9-16).

Ham was controlled by distrust of his father, but Isaac was trusting, and the end result was Ham's descendants were cursed, and Isaac's were blessed.

We can see that one of Satan's major attacks on American society has been the institutionalization of children's lack of respect for their parents. This really took root in the '60s. It is "expected" that teenagers will reject their parent's values and guidance. This is thought of today as a "normal" part of growing up and has led to a culture of individualism. *Teen-age rebellion* !!

Individualism puts "me first", destroys the concept of living for the sake of others and breaks down any vertical connection to God. It can be said that it is the poison that kills free society. *Secular individualism*.

As the vertical connection is dissolved, individualism spreads like cancer and the natural ethics vanish. Big government has to step in with multitudes of rules and regulations, handing over our God given freedoms and allowing ourselves to be ruled "for our own protection". We can see the end result of this trend by looking at any country that has embraced socialism and especially communism. Total loss of freedom and total control by the government, but this is another topic that deserves study by itself.

The point being, that we need to restore the vertical connection by respecting and honoring our parents. We learn to love others and live for a greater whole. By respecting our parents we naturally learn the vertical connection to God our Heavenly Father and biblical ethics become our way of life. The need for government intrusion does not exist and we can live as free and happy people.

Once we have learnt this on an individual level we need to take it to the family level. As Rev Sun Myung Moon said *"Next, you have to become sons of filial piety on the family level before God, centering on purity, pure lineage, and pure love. Your whole family must become children of filial piety, not just you as individuals"*.

Our whole family can act in a filial way. Each generation respecting and honoring the preceding one. This naturally requires purity (following God's original operating instructions given to Adam and Eve – "do not eat of the fruit of the tree of good and evil" Gen 2:16).

As individuals we grow to maturity, become fruitful and then we can join together with our spouse to build our families, and have children of our own. Through this purity our lineage can remain God's and true love can abound.

The next step, once we are on this path, is quite a natural one. We not only respect and honor our parents as filial sons and daughters and as families, but we extend that attitude outwards into society. We live for the sake of our community in small or large ways.

Some have natural leadership talents and become public servants in charge of different aspect of government. Others, at the other extreme serve by cleaning up the trash, with multiple ways to serve in between. Owning a business, being a teacher, driving a bus are all examples of this. Society also benefits immensely from the efforts of volunteers, who form associations of every sort to promote the internal and external welfare of the community - churches, charities, civic clubs, political parties, labor unions, advocacy groups, block associations and self-help groups to name a few.

We love our community and country as the extension of our family. We naturally become patriots of our nation. There are patriots who become more famous than others just by the acts of patriotism they commit.

David was an example from the Old Testament age who remained faithful to Israel even when rejected, and his life threatened, by King Saul.

The Founding Fathers of America sacrificed everything they had to bring freedom to this country, creating a nation under God.

Gandhi and Martin Luther King are more modern examples from closer to our time who both sacrificed personal comfort and their lives to help their country. Both felt the suffering of their people and determined to peacefully free them.

We go beyond patriotism to live for the sake of all mankind.

Saints are motivated by compassion, born of God's love. They can endure suffering and sacrifice because their hearts are full of genuine love for all people. They see things from God's point of view, beyond race, creed and nation. The bible is a record of stories of those who put the greater good of God's coming Kingdom above their own lives. The apostles of Jesus and especially St Paul showed us the way. They were put into the position of following Christ's example of loving and sacrificing for their enemy. The original pattern for this was set in the Old Testament by Jacob when he returned to meet his brother Esau who was determined to kill him. Offering his wealth and treasure with the utmost humility, he moved his brother's heart, and they completely reconciled. (Gen. 33:1-11)

From there we move on to becoming God's representatives.
As Rev Moon said *"From that position, you should become representatives of the owner, representatives who are fully capable of becoming princes and princesses who can inherit the kingship of heaven from the individual level up to the level of the cosmos."* The owner in this sentence is God, the original owner of all creation, who gave the dominion of creation to his children (Gen. 1: 26-28).

Jesus was the first true man to accomplish this and become His representative (John 6:29) *"This is the work of God, that ye believe on him whom he hath sent."* But it is God's desire, and the ultimate destiny, for all mankind to accomplish this through the Messiah. We are all to become kings and queens in the Kingdom of Heaven with the Lord of the 2$^{nd}$ Advent as the King of Kings and Lord of Lords.

Moon

## Summary

To reiterate then we see that by giving us this second pledge, Rev Moon is clearly pointing to God through our vertical connection:
Be filial as individuals and then as families.
Extend that outward into society to become patriots in ways great or small (God sees the heart behind our actions) and outwards again into the world as saints.
And from there to becoming true sons and daughters of God and as such, princes and princesses and kings and queens of the Kingdom of Heaven on earth.
Hallelujah!

## Gaia's Gems for Personal Expansion

### Gaia's Gem 2 – FIDELITY

*Sorry – God-centered origin* [handwritten annotation]

The four position foundation refers to a <u>parent-centered origin of true love</u>. <u>After that, it refers to the perfected parent-child oneness in love</u>. This oneness is not temporary, but <u>eternal and absolute</u>. The origin of this love is unique, unchanging, and absolute. However, love does not exist only in God or only in the father or mother. It come about on the foundation of the *family- a true family!* **Fidelity** *in such a love centered family requires love to be absolute. It is absolute in all its relationships. An invasion in even one of these relationships cannot be allowed because that would mean the destruction of all of them. Thus, each family member within the four –position foundation must guard against the possibility of love being invaded even to the point of self-sacrifice. The most fearful thing is for the foundation of love to be broken. This single nucleus expands to become the world.* (SMM)

Filial = family
Fidelity = obedience in Truth [handwritten note]

# Chapter Three

## Commit yourself and family to grow your heart for God and His Kingdom.

**Our family pledges to perfect the Four Great Realms of Heart, the ~~Three Great Kingships~~ and the ~~Realm of the Royal Famil~~y, by centering on true love.**

*"When we get to Number three, it talks about the Four Great Realms of Heart, the Three Great Kingships, and the realm of the royal family. This is like a textbook, and shows the pattern that should be fulfilled by everyone."* (SMM)

### *The Four Great Realms of Heart*

We say that the purpose of creation was joy – the emotional satisfaction that comes from true love. God made the physical creation in order to experience the fullness of true love with His object partners, His children. This is why emotion and love are the strongest forces in creation. This emotional impulse is referred to as "heart".

God's heart is the irrepressible Source from which all love flows. Our hearts, created in the image of God, are created to be the same but need to first receive God's love and then grow to pass it on.

God's heart can be described as an irrepressible emotional impulse welling up from deep within Himself that seeks joy by sharing love with His object partner. God created human beings in His image and likeness that we might become His objects of love. Thus, as the image of God, it is our original nature to interact with others in love.

The four great realms of heart then, are four areas, or realms, of our capacity to love.

Pledge number three of the Family Pledge is referring to the unfallen original world before the fall. It is talking about returning to that original world. The entire process of growth we undergo – for example from babyhood all the way through parenthood – all of this is keyed towards finding our position as a spouse and a parent. The goal is to find that position which allows us to become one body with God fulfilling the original purpose of creation. The perfection of the Four Great Realms of Heart is the path we have to go to perfect ourselves as human beings.

By allowing us to multiply and give birth to our own children, God allows us to experience, as His creation in His image, the position of a creator ourselves, stimulation flowing back from our own substantial creation. Thus, the family is the foundation which allows us to experience, from generation to generation, the four great realms of child's heart, sibling's heart, the couple's heart and the parent's heart, and to grow to perfection in each of those realms.    4 realms ♡:   child ♡
                                                           sibling ♥
                                                           couple ♀♂
                                                           parent ♥

That is why the family is a starting point of perfection through which we can achieve the unity of God and mankind in love, and come to own heaven and earth. In other words, the family becomes the original starting point for the ideal children, siblings, couples and parents. It is only from this place that men and women with united minds and bodies can emerge, and it is only here that we can see a couple who have perfected the ideal of husband–wife unity, or the start of the ideal parents. Furthermore, this is the place where, centering on true love, the model for the perfection of children, siblings, couples and parents can be created.

The hope of God is to rejoice together with mankind in the kingdom of God. Heavenly Father's heart finds its complete fulfillment when human beings achieve their true purpose: perfecting the four great realms of heart and becoming the image of God as His sons and daughters, sharing love and beauty with God, and multiplying into families, societies, nations and a world which moves in harmony and unity according to the mind of God. Every individual human being who stimulates God with joy has a heart which resonates in tune with God's heart. He lives in oneness with God, for "God is love, and he who abides in love abides in God, and God abides in him." (1 John 4:16) The world which moves in unity with the purpose of God's heart stimulates God with eternal joy and delight. (Isa. 62:4) Such a world will be called *the Kingdom of Heaven*.

## *The Three Great Kingships*

Families that have completed and perfected the Four Great Realms of Heart and Three Great Kingships are ideal families. In those families, the grandfather is like God, the parents are the king and queen of the families of the world, and the children, are the kings and queens of the future, who inherit the kingship of both earth and heaven. God holds the kingship over heaven, and the parents hold the kingship over the earth. The sons and daughters are the kings and queens who inherit this. Thus, the place where these Three Great Kingships are bound together and bear fruit is our own ideal family.

The three generations are together one unit, one category, and this is why we have to attend our grandparents like we attend God, to attend our parents like the king and queen of the world, and the grandchildren, we have to attend like they are the kings and queens of the Kingdom of Heaven and earth that will come in the future.

So we can say then that the kingships described by Rev Moon are referring to a tradition of true love inherited from generation to generation. In the secular world, the royal office descends from father to the eldest son but due to the fall of Adam and Eve this position was claimed by Satan. Restoration calls for it to pass to the youngest son claiming the role of elder. The traditions of royalty are passed on as the prince receives his education in the future duties of his office. The kingship of true love likewise includes traditions of altruism, selflessness, forgiveness, sacrifice and public service, passed down from generation to generation. Having achieved kingship by maturing through the Four Great Realms of Heart, true parents then guide the next generation to follow true love's way through the Four Great Realms of Heart. When this tradition has continued through three generations in the family - grandparents, parents and children - kingship has been securely established in that family. It can then be called a royal family of true love. For this reason, the Family Pledge calls us to perfect the *Three* Great *Kingships,* meaning kingship in three consecutive generations of the family.

For an example of such a godly family tradition in the history of God's providence, Abraham, Isaac and Jacob were three generations who established the foundations of faith and substance and became the root of the people of Israel. Their family tradition included faith in God, moral virtue, respect for parents, and forgiveness for their brother. Each generation had to have such faith in God as to migrate to a strange land. Each generation cherished the blessing which God gave their parents and overcame trials in order to realize it. Joseph carried on this proud tradition when he went to Egypt. He overcame the temptation of Potiphar's wife, forgave his eleven brothers who sold him into slavery, and honored his father Jacob.

Three generations are necessary to establish a solid tradition that can overcome the wrong habits which we have inherited from the human Fall. The Fall occurred through three generations: God representing the grandparents' position, Adam and Eve, and their children Cain and Abel. The proper relationships between these three generations were broken, and all suffered as a result. God lost the respect of His children, and the authority of His love was spurned. Adam and Eve corrupted their love and betrayed their Father in heaven. Cain and Abel carried on in the false and self-centered tradition of love set by Adam and Eve to the point of murder. To restore this false tradition, three generations of kingship should be set up in each family in order for it to qualify as a royal family of true love.

## *The Kingship of Grandparents*

Grandparents are kings and queens representing the past, the spirit world and God. Having pioneered the way of love and having attained true parenthood, they own a treasure-store of wisdom and experience. They have set the tradition of love, and this serves as the basis of their authority for subsequent generations. We should be grateful for the tradition which our grandparents established for us. As representatives of the spirit world, all our ancestors are honored through them.

Grandparents have particular value for what they can teach others, especially their grandchildren. Even in our inner cities, where the plague of drugs has destroyed a generation of families, children can find protection and guidance from their grandparents to compensate for their parents' failure. Statistics show that the presence of a loving grandfather and grandmother can often save the children of single mothers from a life of crime. Grandparents even adopt their grandchildren when the parents' family falls apart. They provide their grandchildren with the values and stability which the parents lacked. All children need their grandparents to receive the love and wisdom to which they are entitled. When grandchildren gather around their grandparents, they feel warm acceptance, joy and love.

For their part, the grandparents find great joy in loving their grandchildren. Their authority as kings and queens entitles them to appreciation and support by all the members of the family. Even though their bodies may be weak and frail, there are many roles in the home for them to contribute to the welfare of the family. Whether baby-sitting, cooking or tending the garden, <u>many opportunities</u> exist for <u>grandparents to continue experiencing the joy of giving. By no means should we ever send them to languish in an old age home.</u>

How do our grandparents represent God? <u>Even physically, the white hair of the aged symbolizes God.</u> In the family of the first ancestors, Adam and Eve, God was the grandfather. God longed to love His grandchildren, Cain and Abel; but His love was blocked due to the Fall. In restoration, the broken family of three generations God, Adam and Eve, and Cain and Abel - are restored by the three generations of grandparents, parents and children. God longs to recover the love He missed in Adam's family through the experience of grandparents. In Rev Sun Myung Moon's family, he as grandfather represents God, his son, as his heir and successor, Hyung Jin Moon is the king of the present, and Shin Gil Moon as the grandson is the king of the future. With these three great kingships, the foundation for the Kingdom of Heaven will be accomplished and God's heart greatly relieved.

## *The Kingship of Parents*

<u>Parents are kings and queens representing the present. They lead the family with love and set the tone for its spiritual life. They are responsible for the family's material welfare, providing both for their children and their aged parents, and setting the example of the proper way of the father and mother roles.</u>

We have already discussed at length the meaning of kingship and of the value and authority of the subject partner's love. This well describes the kingship of parents. By virtue of their warm love and clear teaching of norms, cultivated through the Four Great Realms of Heart, they guide their family and raise their children. By their sacrifice for the welfare of their community, nation and world, they command the respect from everyone around them. At the same time, the respect they receive in the larger community enhances their authority and honor at home.

Clearly, it takes hard work and great investment for a parent to be worthy of the title of king and queen. First, they must cut off any fallen habits and attitudes. They must deepen their spirituality to meet God, who wants to dwell within them. By realizing their true, original selves, they can become true leaders of others. Living in oneness with God, their love becomes patient, kind and uplifting, while at the same time totally unafraid to expose and denounce the ways of Satan in this world. We see from Jesus' example how he was ready to forgive those who had a repentful heart, cure those who were sick, spent hours and days teaching about God's Kingdom to those ready to listen, but took a whip to the money changers in God's temple.

## Children as Kings and Queens of the future

Children represent the future. One day they *will* become parents and take on the central responsibility for their families. One day they will perfect the Four Great Realms of Heart and attain the kingship of love. In a sense, they are princes and princesses being trained to assume kingship in the future.

We should give our children a positive and challenging sense of what it means to be a true child. We should train them to have a higher standard of behavior and better character. We should let them understand that they should prepare themselves for a challenging life, for many of them will be called as the nation's future leaders.

How do parents train their children to have the qualities of nobility, courage, honor and compassion? How do parents teach them faith and knowledge of God? How do parents instill in them a sense of public responsibility? By far the most important lesson is by the parents' own example. Children are great imitators; they learn from example. Regardless of what parents say, it is by their deeds that their children take the lesson. This follows from what has been said about the children's realm of heart, where love grows only as induced by the parents' love. Next in importance is the parents' conscious training of the children and the expectations they instill in them by their words.

Even children exercise a sort of kingship. Children often take the subject position in the family. What small baby does not coax the love from her mother with a smile, a laugh, or a twinkling eye? Rev. Moon once remarked that when a father bends over to kiss his baby, it is like bowing to a king. As the children grow, they have needs which cry out for their parents' attention.

Children need a proper education in norms and values. This is their right, and any parent would be remiss in not attending to this need. As the children demonstrate filial piety in loving their parents and siblings, their parents respond with praise and encouragement. This fosters in the child a measure of self-respect.

The child's opinions also need to be taken seriously. Who knows, perhaps God speaks through him? After all, each child bears a small cosmos within himself. The child should be given a measure of freedom in order to experience the consequences of his actions. These are only a few of the ways in which children's love carries with it the authority and value of kingship.

Jesus blessed the children, saying, "Let the children come to me, and do not hinder them; for to such belongs the kingdom of God." (Mark 10:14)

We indeed place our trust in our children, for they will have the opportunity to build the Kingdom of God on the foundations we have laid. We hope and expect that our children will surpass us.

Nevertheless, our children have their own free will and portion of responsibility, and nothing is certain. Therefore, as parents, we tremble before the responsibility of raising children. We pour out our love to bring our children to the point where they can claim their birthright as citizens of the Kingdom of God.

### *The realm of Royal Family*

It was mentioned above that a royal family of true love is established when a firm tradition has been laid through the

<u>Three Great Kingships</u>. This means that three successive generations mature through the Four Great Realms of Heart to attain the kingship of true love. Each generation completes its Four Position Foundation. Each embodies a love imbued with authority that elicits honor and respect. Each passes down the tradition of true love to the next generation.

<u>A family is completed in three generations</u>. Furthermore, as was mentioned above, three generations are needed to restore the Fall, when three generations were lost. Let us now examine these points in greater detail.

With the Fall, the three generations of God, Adam and Eve, and Cain and Abel became separated from God's ideal and established a satanic family tradition rather than God's royal family tradition. Their descendants, all humankind, have been part of Satan's lineage. None of the royal families on earth have been God's royal family.

*So why no children?*

<u>God's royal family began with Jesus Christ</u>, of whom it is said, "at the name of Jesus every knee should bow, in heaven and on earth and under the earth, and every tongue confess that Jesus Christ is Lord, to the glory of God the Father." (Phil. 2:10-11)

Jesus after his resurrection established God's reign in heaven, while asking us to pray that the Kingdom of God come on earth. (Matt. 6:10)
The Messiah reigns as the "King of kings and Lord of lords." (Rev. 19:16)

Christ is the head of the Church, and by participating in the body of Christ we grow up to be like the head, inheriting the spirit and life of Christ in ourselves. (Eph. 4:12-16)

Satan had been our false father and ruler. Fallen habits, fallen attitudes, and fallen ways of life remain deeply ingrained in us. Having entered this realm, we should forget everything we ever knew about life and start again as young children, learning everything afresh, as Jesus said, "whoever does not receive the kingdom of God like a child cannot enter it." (Luke 18:17). Nevertheless, our deeply-ingrained habits and attitudes cannot so easily be removed.

For this world to be changed at its core, leaders must arise who know true love and the laws of God. Who might they be? No one is better qualified than we ourselves, who know God and true family values. Every one of us should emerge as a leader in his family, displaying the brilliant light of true love for all to see. At least some should rise up to become their communities' leading citizens. One may be elected mayor; another may open a soup kitchen to help the homeless. Nothing is impossible; whatever efforts we make in true love will eventually bear fruit. A few blessed families will even rise to become presidents and first ladies of our nations.

*unmarried, & childless = outside the Royal (Holy) Family of God.*

As long as there are people remaining outside the Realm of the Royal Family, they are still under Satan's bondage. This means the pain is not entirely healed in the heart of God - who looks for even one lost lamb even though the ninety-nine other sheep are safe. (Luke 14:37) When countless families fulfill their responsibility to live by true love, the entire population of the earth and all its lands will belong to the Realm of the Royal Family. When every last person is included, it will mean the end of Satan's royal family. This will bring complete liberation to God's heart. It will also mean the end of Satan, who will no longer have any base upon which to influence humanity.

So what is the "realm of the royal family"? "The realm of the royal family" expresses the intention to save all the people of the satanic world. We should love those people like our own younger brothers and sisters and enter the Kingdom of Heaven taking them along with us. What we have to remember here is that we have to bring them along with us. We cannot go alone.

## *Summary*

This pledge is for us to grow through the 4 great realms of heart within our family, perfecting the child's love, sibling love, couple's love and parents love.

We create the 3 great kingships of the past, present and future, restoring what was God's original desire.

And knowing that Heavenly Father cannot be happy as long as anyone is separated from Him, bring Satan's children back to Him and into heaven with us.

---

### Gaia's Gems for Personal Expansion

Gaia Gem 3 - ESSENCE

*Do NOT live in the past or the future — but only in the present.*

BE present in the present time. Aware of what you are experiencing and how you feel. Be present while others communicate with you about their intention.

Release resistances. Change prospective from fearful to loving. See others as spiritual beings and not as separated personalities. We are all God's children.

I COMMIT TO FEEL GENUINE LOVE EVERYDAY ALL THE TIME in which ever realm I am.

# Chapter Four

## Commit yourself and family to the one world family of God.

**Our family, pledges to build the universal family encompassing heaven and earth, which is God's ideal of creation, and perfect the world of freedom, peace, unity and happiness, by centering on true love.**

*"Family number four states: "Our family... pledges to build the universal family encompassing heaven and earth, which is God's ideal of creation, and perfect the world of freedom, peace, unity and happiness, by centering on true love"! It is from here that happiness arises. Happiness, freedom and the ideal are realized in the family of the ideal of creation desired by God." (SMM)*

*"What is Family number four? It pertains to the universal family encompassing heaven and earth. All human beings are brothers and sisters – one lineage. We must protect it like God. Even though we are sitting in His royal palace, we must fulfill pledge number four. We must form the universal family and realize the world of freedom, peace, unity and happiness. I have such a heart. I am an advocate of the universal family. I must plant freedom, happiness, unity and peace. What does this mean? It is to reveal my history. It is the ultimate goal of my life. You should know it clearly." (SMM)*

## *The Universal family*

In the beginning God created the world with the ideal of true Love. If Adam and Eve had not fallen, their family would have multiplied and become one extended family throughout the world. It would have become a peaceful world of the Adamic cultural realm. Accordingly, at the conclusion of the history of restoration, a true family based on true parents and true love will be established as the hope of humankind and at the same time, the hope of God. This true family will serve as the source of true love and true life and the starting point of the peace and happiness of humankind. It's a great family.

It is formed through the establishment of the realm of the royal unfallen family. Through the standard of peace whereby the members of the royal family are connected, they should become a kinship possessing the friendship and love of the great fraternity of the cosmos. They are to form the universal family encompassing heaven and earth. Then, since that family has been formed, God will also enjoy freedom and peace. God and His sons and daughters will not be obstructed. Freedom and peace will not be obstructed and unity will not be obstructed.

I was speaking with a good church friend the other day and he shared with me his testimony of meeting the messiah, and I thought what a great example of the Universal family. I would like to share it with you.
He was camping in the Colorado wilderness. In his late teens, he was desperately asking God for the direction he should take with his life, hoping that the answer would be to become a recluse as he didn't really like people that

much. God, however had a different idea. God showed him an ant hill and told him that this was a model for the kingdom of heaven. All the ants were busy working together for the betterment of the whole, helping each other as needed and all living a happy fulfilled life, lacking nothing. Some were building the ant hill, others were out gathering food. When needed, some would gather together to create a bridge for others to bring food across. And all were ready to defend the hill from outside threats.

Shortly after, he left the wilderness, went to San Francisco and met some people who helped him find Christ.

In the Universal Family each individual will be connected to the rest through the kinship of being one family under God, happy to help others and work for the whole. Just as in the ant community, some will be builders, some food gatherers, some leaders and some peace police protecting us from danger. All of us able to follow our heart and use our creativity to help others.

In this ideal society all people will transcend nationality and race to engage in mutual cooperation, create harmony and live in happiness. This community is that of the extended family in which all people are conscious of being the sons and daughters of the one God.

The society of the ideal world will be characterized politically by principles of interdependence, economically by mutual prosperity and ethically by universally shared values. The core content of the principle of interdependence is co-ownership based on God's true love.

The basic model of the society of interdependence is the family. By co-ownership, I do not mean ownership merely in relation to material possessions, but ownership based on God's love. We have seen historically where this concept can lead when not based on God but on Satan with the advent of socialism and especially communism.

In the family, even though all property would be legally held in the parents' names, in practice it would be jointly owned by the parents and children; that is, by the whole family. At the same time, the individual family members are allocated their own rooms, clothing and allowances. In this way, in the family, the whole purpose and the individual purpose are harmonized. When this ideal form of ownership of the family, based on such love, expands to the society, nation and world, it becomes the form of ownership of the ideal society.

In this ideal society, the whole purpose and the individual purpose are naturally harmonized. Since human beings also have desires and the autonomy of love, they also pursue individual ownership and individual purpose. Even so, they do not pursue unlimited individual possession or an individual purpose that undermines the whole purpose. Perfected human beings are meant to own property commensurate with their position and circumstances according to their conscience and original nature.

In particular, since the economic activity of ideal human beings – who have the character of true owners of all things by virtue of true love – would manifest love and gratitude, there can be no avarice or corruption. At the same time, there could be no emphasis on regional or national interests inconsistent with the purpose of the whole, and economic activity will have its aim and focus not in the pursuit of profits but rather in overall welfare. In the government, the major organs and departments of the ideal nation are harmonized through a smooth give and take action with one another under their common purpose. This is similar to the various organs of the human body, which work together for a common purpose according to the commands of the brain. The government bureaucracies we see in operation today could be viewed as a form of cancer where the cells grow out of control, centered on themselves at the expense of the whole.

### *The world of freedom, peace, unity and happiness.*

Family Pledge number four states that we will become God's global and universal family and realize the world of freedom, peace, unity and happiness. Isn't that what the four great realms of heart are all about?

Even when we have realized the four great realms of heart in our family, this will not be the end of it. We have the responsibility to bring the world back to God through that family. We have to take care of the insecurities and anxieties of the world, the chaos caused by the satanic way, and the unhappy environment that is not free, not at peace and certainly not united.

In the last chapter we spoke about the realm of the royal family where we win the hearts of those in the satanic realm and bring them with us into the kingdom of heaven. It means that we should realize an extended family conforming to God's ideal and as such, we cannot exclude the satanic world. This doesn't mean including satanic ways but by becoming the kings and queens spoken about in the previous chapter, having accomplished the four great realms of heart, we bring together everyone from the satanic world as an extended family and allow them stand in the place of freedom, peace, unity and happiness. For there to be freedom and peace, unity must be included. Our ideal is peace and unity. We will achieve unity by winning and assimilating those following the fallen way and separating them from Satan. *Don't give up on non-believers & keep @ it.*

The saints who have come and gone until now have only thought about how to unify the external world. Many time they would have to sacrifice some major part of their life such as external belongings and even marital love. However, what is different now is that we are also concerned about the individual internal aspects and how we can maintain unity first there. Without unity, there is neither peace nor freedom. Happiness and freedom come only on the basis of unity. Unity is most important. If your mind and body are not united can you truly be free or feel happy? *& become a Saint?*

When your mind and body clash, is there happiness? Isn't this why you are agonizing over your life? This is fundamentally the big question. Where is happiness or peace when your mind and body are disunited? All problems arise from this.

Communists and people like Marx and Hegel observed that the mind and body struggle, and thus thought that this was the basic aspect of humanity. They did not know that this happened because of the Fall and the resulting satanic influence. This is where the concept of struggle originated and the socialist / communist concept of violent revolution being necessary for progress to take place. We see the fruits of this with the political left stirring up violent protests and riots at every opportunity, believing that this is the way to a better world.

We need to fully realize that where there is no unity there can be no peace and happiness. This starts within ourselves and extends outwards. St. Paul spoke of this in Galatians 5:13-26 encouraging us to be free by walking in the spirit and not having give and take with the lusts of the flesh. As we have been called to freedom, don't use it as an opportunity to go after the desires of the flesh but to love one another and love our neighbor as our self. I have found that when I am most struggling, I can overcome best by finding ways to serve others – helping someone with a project they are working on, or cleaning the church for example.

This leads to well-balanced and loving people. Individuals living in this fashion are much better equipped to create a united family. St. Paul gave us excellent guidance on the way to create unity of husband and wife in Ephesians 5:21-33 with the wife loving and respecting her husband as if he represents Christ and the husband loving his wife as if she were his own body, both being told to put their spouse beyond their own personal desires. When the wife testifies to the greatness of her husband and the husband unconditionally loves his wife, and the two of them learn not to react with negative emotions to each other, the children, nurtured by this caring environment, can easily love and unite with them and each other. With this family as the building block of society, we can see how unity can bring peace in an ever expanding realm.

We need to keep in mind that if God's love and our human love do not come from the same origin, they will diverge and the unity we speak of will not occur. It is critical that we learn to see things from God's point of view and love accordingly.

Had the Fall not taken place, how would Adam's family, formed through true love, have propagated itself? Adam and Eve would have become ideal true spouses. Next, they would have become true parents, and then the true ancestors of their descendants and all humankind in accordance with true love. Human beings multiplying from Adam and Eve as their true parents would have formed an extended family and thereby a peaceful world of the Adamic cultural sphere.

Accordingly, the culmination of the history of restoration lies in establishing the true family based on true parents and true love as the hope of humankind and at the same time the hope of God. This true family will serve as the source of true love and true life and the starting point of the freedom, peace and happiness of humankind. The role of the True Parent is the second coming of Christ that He promised to us, and will usher in the Kingdom of Heaven on earth. *Now "True Mother" is the old lady in Pennsylvania Not the old, True Mother.*

However, this requires the complete effort, victory and separation form Satan of both the Father and the Mother. We are now witnessing firsthand the misery, suffering and chaos caused when after the total victory of the Father, the Mother decides to push aside his victory and directions and go her own way, glorifying herself as an empress. Unfortunately, although she is calling for unity centering

*Han mother - True mother old, True mother*

on herself, that unity cannot be established unless it is based 100% on God and His ideals. *Not worldly ideas.*

**Summary**

To conclude then, we are pledging to build God's ideal – the universal family. This is the where *all* human beings are *conscious* of being a son or daughter of God. We feel it to the fullest extent of our hearts. We can achieve unity through true love and can build a world of freedom, peace and happiness.

Gaia's Gems for Personal Expansion

Gaia Gem 4 - APPRECIATION

*I commit to live with integrity and from my* inner *essence.*

Stop focusing on problems or other issues, rather focus only on expressing appreciations to your partner or to anyone else you want to be close to.

Choose a heartfelt commitment to making the expression of appreciation your top creative priority.

Notice things to appreciate in your partner and or family members, mainly verbal appreciations, and deliver to each and all ten or twenty time a day.

Most people find that expressing appreciation clears up even long-standing, recurring problems that nothing else has helped before.

Choose appreciation as your highest art form.

AKA { *If you cannot say something nice, then choose to say nothing at all.*

# Chapter Five

## Commit yourself and family to uniting His Kingdom.

**Our family, pledges to strive every day to advance the unification of the spirit world and the physical world as subject and object partners, by centering on true love.**

*"You should know that the universal family possesses the spirit world and physical world. If we are to realize an extended family, we should unify God's Kingdom on earth and in heaven. We have such a mission. "Our family pledges to strive every day to advance the unification of the spirit world and the physical world as subject and object partners, by centering on true love!" This is daily, once a day and not once a year. It states that the spirit world is the subject partner every day. There is the spirit world – the heavenly nation. Next, there is the physical world as the object partner. Then what? We strive to advance the unification. So without resting, we should have stimulation and excitement to develop their unification. There is no time to rest. If we want to be an extended family of the spirit world, we must unify heaven and earth." (SMM)*

When we die, we enter the spirit world. So we must solve the problems of the spirit world on earth before we go. We cannot just go to the spirit world and find ourselves caught by its laws. Everything must be resolved on earth. Our limited time here in the physical world is a preparation for our passing over to the eternal world of spirit. This is not a concept but a reality. Once we sense such a spirit world to be real, we need have no problem with persecutions, however many. If opposition and persecution are concepts, this is a reality. Only then will we stay alive. The most important thing is how to have a real experience of the existence of the spirit world. Once we do, persecution is not a problem. This is so because we know our purpose. When arising in the morning, we should have greater awareness of the reality of the spirit world than the facts of nature. Spirit world then becomes the subject to our object physical life. However, we should not focus on the spirit world at the cost of our physical lives, but get our priorities straight, living our physical lives according to the spiritual laws of true love.

I was working at a festival just last weekend. Backstage there was a coffee stand run by a young lady. Although the coffee was a very high quality, there was no charge for all the staff and performers. I had some good natured bantering with the young lady and thanked her for the wonderful coffee. She responded by commenting on how happy she felt bringing so many people joy by giving them free coffee and said wouldn't it be nice to give joy to others on a daily basis. She had realized a very great spiritual truth just by giving out coffee! We can live lives of true love bringing joy to others in everything we do, even the simplest things, and by so doing, grow our spirits in preparation for eternity.

Being vast, the spirit world does not just have Koreans, Japanese, Britons and Americans. People of diverse nationalities of the same spiritual level congregate together. All five races are gathered in one place. Whether we are Americans or other nationals, we will still recognize the human form we used to see in the past, but since we see the world of the heart, how beautiful the world of our heart is will determine how close we can be to people. We will want to gather together with people whose world of heart is the most beautiful. We will be together as one even if we are told not to be and we will instantaneously recognize people from millennia or tens of millennia ago as soon as we meet them.

For this reason it is very good for us to travel and visit other neighborhoods and countries than our own. When we can freely travel the world and relate to peoples of all different countries and continents, we are preparing ourselves for our future eternal life.

God called me out of England many years ago and took me on a trail of adventure through Europe and into the Middle East. This was an amazing experience of different cultures, peoples and even foods. I was at the tender age of 20 and it changed my life forever as I quickly learned that external appearances were really unimportant. What mattered was the heart of people.

In today's world we tend to think of spirit world just as a concept or dream, and not something real. What is important is whether we can sense it tangibly rather than just conceptually. If we can comprehend that, we will see that this physical world is but a shadow of the spirit world. As that world has no borders, if we have a loving heart there, we will be able to relate to everyone we meet.

The mind does not age. The older it is, the more beautiful it becomes. So would it be good if God's sons and daughters all looked ugly in the spirit world? No. Those who live in the harmony of deep love will all become beautiful people. This is true not just of women but also men. Had Adam and Eve not fallen in the Garden of Eden, they would have lived with God and reflected God's beauty. Our life in the physical world is a preparation for our eternal life.

In the original purpose of creation, Adam's body was created by God to be His physical representation. God, the creator and an invisible spiritual being, wanted Adam's body in order to experience true love. It is through Christ (the restoration of fallen Adam) that God can at last have this experience and there can now be communication with the spirit world. It is not God Himself who fulfills His love, but rather through human beings. Through the Lord at His Second Advent the barriers between the spirit world and physical world are broken down, communication can take place and true love can flow.

I think it important that we understand the stages of growth to better understand the relationship of our physical bodies and spiritual bodies.

The spirit comes into existence at the time of conception. It has been captured on video that there is a flash of light or burst of energy when the sperm penetrates the egg and the two unite.

This is now the formation stage as both the spirit and body are created as the cells divide and grow into the form of a baby. This is life in water and our experience is one of being completely surrounded, protected and bathed in the love of our mother. All our needs are provided by our mother physically through the umbilical cord. After a specific time period we go through a traumatic occurrence called birth. We are thrust out into the world of air, the umbilical cord is cut, and we have to start doing things for our self – breathing and eating to name but 2. This is the growth period. Just as our body grows to adult hood and beyond so does our spirit. Our body requires nutrition and air in order to grow and in the same way our spirit needs the same. The air for our spirit is the freely given love of God. The nutrition is given by the body to the spirit in the form of vitality elements. These vitality elements can be good or bad and depend on the actions of our physical mind and body. Good deeds, having faith and following God's word, loving and caring for others all lead to good vitality elements flowing to our spirit, bringing growth toward a beautiful and vibrant spiritual being of true love that can relate freely with God. Selfish and destructive thoughts and deeds send bad vitality elements to our spirit causing us to become stunted and ugly. It was for this reason that Christ came to earth to forgive our sins and open the way for us to change our hearts and thereby our actions. Through accepting, believing and living with Christ we can become the good spiritual beings desired by God. This can only happen while our spirits are living within our physical bodies. It was for this reason that Christ said to Peter when he gave him the keys to the Kingdom of Heaven *"whatever you bind on earth shall be bound in heaven, and whatever you loose on earth shall be loosed in heaven."*

We then go through another traumatic occurrence called death when we leave our physical bodies behind and our spirit goes to live for eternity in the spiritual world with God. This is the completion stage. Where we go in spirit world is not determined by God but by ourselves and our actions during our physical life.

This brings us back around to the relationship of our spirit self and physical self and why we pledge to strive every day to advance the unification of the spirit world and the physical world as subject and object partners, by centering on true love.

---

## Gaia's Gems for Personal Expansion

### Gaia's Gem 5 – ALIGNMENT

We are moving into an expanded awareness in this 21 Century. It reminds us that we are larger than any circumstances around us. There are many ways to come into vertical alignment where body, mind and spirit are connected. Such practices as meditation, prayer, yoga, or even simple walks in nature are the adjustments we need to make. Nature is a wonderful model of what we are, but often forget - physical vessels through which God's infinite divine energy flows, and is always available. We are never alone. God's spirit grows in and with us.

Our personal seeking or awareness of this can help to heal the separation between mind and body, and with our positive personal choices, the spiritual world and the physical world can emerge united. In this state we can feel

more balanced, resourceful, held safe and calm; and we can
shift from the confusion caused by the overwhelm of the external world into a more resilient and clear experience.

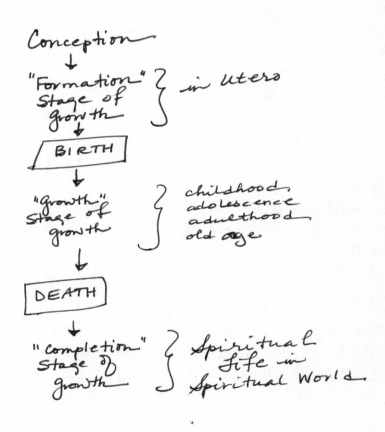

# Chapter Six

## Commit yourself and family to spreading Heavenly Fortune.

**Our family pledges to become a family that moves heavenly fortune by embodying God and True Parents, and to become a family that conveys Heaven's blessing to our community, by centering on true love.**

*We must be families representing God and work to bring peace, happiness and freedom on the earth. So we should always move in rhythm with heaven and earth. Next, since we are in rhythm with God as a family, we should be a family that can transmit heavenly fortune to our communities. This is Pledge number six. By such means, we eventually become a family that embodies God and True Parents and achieve the unified realm of God's heart. The world of the culture of heart begins today throughout the world. This is our pledge. (SMM)*

In the beginning Adam and Eve were supposed to believe in God and His word, grow to maturity and perfection (be fruitful), multiply (have children and create a family) and take dominion over the creation as God the creator's children (Gen 1:28). By so doing, they would have become the True Parents of mankind, the original human ancestors embodying God, from whom all of mankind would have come, creating one universal family, the lineage of God and the Kingdom of Heaven on earth. This did not happen due to the fall, and Adam and Eve became the fallen human ancestors embodying sin, creating a world of suffering, division and misery, the world and lineage of Satan. As Jesus said in John 8:44 "you are of your father the devil".

The goal of restoration is for the Messiah to come and restore that position, bringing the promise of True Parents and the lineage of God into reality. We have discussed this in previous chapters.

The Lord of the Second Advent victoriously defeats Satan, takes a bride from Satan's realm and restores her to the position of unfallen Eve. The LSA, having been given the name of True Parents by God, sows his seed in the womb of the restored Eve and God's lineage is now alive on the earth. *Lord of 2ND Advent (Rev. Father Moon)*

By being blessed in marriage by the True Parents we are all given the opportunity to become true parents ourselves. The difference between the True Parents and ourselves is that the LSA has to realize the *global* Kingdom of Heaven, but we just have to realize the *family* Kingdom of Heaven. *Lord of 2ND Advent.*

What does Family Pledge number six state? It states "Our family pledges... to embody God and True Parents..."
We must become families that embody God and True Parents. What does this mean? We might find ourselves thinking how could little me embody someone as huge as God?

As the creator and origin of all things, God can be as small as the tiniest particle and as large as the universe. Everything is created in His image after all. Especially mankind (Gen 1:26). We say that the creation is the indirect image of God, but mankind is the direct image.

There is a beautiful lake in a state park close to my house. My wife and I love to go for walks along the lake shore. We are always moved by the majesty and beauty of the water, trees and creation we see there. The clouds and sky are a constantly changing masterpiece, expressing emotions as varied as peaceful tranquility and tremendous power. Being together, Gaia and I are able to feel God's love and our own love for each other mixed into one, filling us to the brim, refreshing us. We can go back out into the world embodying God ready to give and care for others.

In this way, we can realize a family that conveys God's blessings into our community rather than taking from it. We can become a family that "bring the plus" to our community. If there are people around us who do not understand God's heart and desire, we can teach it to them, even if they oppose us, by both word and deed. We can teach it to our community and gradually expand outward. By living in this way, we will not live alone, but as part of the universal family previously discussed.

One thing that was lost at the fall was unity – unity between God and His children, unity between husband and wife, unity between Cain and Abel (the children), unity between Adam and Eve and the rest of creation and unity between mind and body. We have discussed the importance of unity previously but it plays a part here as well. As with all things claimed by Satan through the fall, restoration back to God has to take place if we are to embody Him. We start on the individual level by regaining unity of mind and body. The mind, centering on God should be the subject, guiding the actions of our body. We need to train ourselves to ask "what would God think" in everything we do to the point where it becomes the automatic way of life. By embodying God in this way, we will be able to take care of our own selves, love our brothers and sisters, unite as husband and wife and bring joy to God.

Instead of selfishly using and trashing the creation around us, we would be sensitive to its needs, becoming heavenly stewards, thereby bringing heavenly fortune.

Humankind must know the way through which heavenly fortune comes. Heavenly fortune is something that moves eternally. It travels along the eternal path, which goes around and around without changing, according to eternal principles. As it shapes and paves the roads of prosperity and decline while going around and around within the relationships of humankind, the question is how we human beings standing here can adapt ourselves to this.

Who controls heavenly fortune? The Lord who created the universe controls it. Who is that Lord? In religious terms we call Him God and use other various nouns, but this is not the issue. There should be a certain Central Being. If we know for sure that the Central Being exists and unshakably follow His path, everything will go well.

Heavenly fortune never perishes. Our life sometimes becomes sidetracked by the environment and flows away along byways, but heavenly fortune does not change its course because it obeys God's governance. It is eternal.

Just as the four seasons of spring, summer, autumn and winter are immutable, the way of heavenly fortune, which moves humankind, moves along the unchanging track relating to human individuals, families, tribes, people, nations and the world. Humankind has been hitherto ignorant of this.

Just as individuals have fortune, so do families, nations, and the world; in the same token, all of heaven and earth has heavenly fortune. However good the fortune we may have been born with, if our family fortune declines, we will suffer hardship together, and also those who may have good individual or family fortunes will not be able to avoid their downfall if the broader national fortune wanes. Moreover, the fortunes of the nation and the world are determined in accordance with the direction and progress of heavenly fortune, which encompasses and exists for the sake of the whole. To establish the heavenly way in the world means to adjust the course of individuals and nations to the path of heavenly fortune.

If we want to ride on heavenly fortune, we first have to know what kind of place the way of heavenly fortune is. It is not a place everybody likes and where we enjoy ourselves eating, drinking and being merry. It can be a place we dislike, but it should be a place where we are always grateful for everything that we are given, and give glory to God while carrying out our responsibilities. Those who stand in such a place can ride on heavenly fortune. A gnat on the rump of a swift stallion travels a great distance even while sucking blood. That is how it is. If we stick to heavenly fortune and don't fall off, everything will be okay.

It will be no good if we just want to receive our own portion of blessing, and then go to the spirit world. Rather, we should accomplish something on earth. We should pass on something that can satisfy everyone and bring them the great benefits of heavenly fortune before we go.

Family Pledge number six states, "Our family pledges to become a family that moves heavenly fortune by embodying God and True Parents, and to perfect a family that conveys Heaven's blessing to our community, by centering on true love!" We are pledging to become wellsprings of blessings to our communities and all those around us.

We are not meant to live comfortably just by ourselves, pursuing external success. That is not what God is like. That is not what parents are like. Even in the fallen world, parents want their sons and daughters to be better off than themselves. Unfortunately, in today's society, external success has become the goal focused on by too many. Children, parents and family are sacrificed and pushed to the side.

Heavenly fortune and blessings however, are God's love and truth. There has been a vast outpouring of this in these last days and all we need to do is ask, seek and knock and it will be given to us (Luke 11:9-10). We can then convey these blessings to those around us and by so doing bring heavenly fortune to our community.

# Gaia's Gems for Personal Expansion

## Gaia's Gem 6 - PARTNERSHIP
Choose to <u>partner with your Higher Power - Your Heavenly Father - God</u>
You need to commit and be absolute in your choices.
<u>Your choices can create constructive consequences or destructive consequence</u>. In your life experience you need to be very aware of your stand in relation with others, because spiritual partnerships are not available to the spiritual tourist or casual shopper. It requires participation and vulnerability with the joint experiment and sometimes bold venture, into the eternally new territory of the eternal present moment.

*"<u>You feel true happiness only when you can feel the heart of your partner and love your partner in an equal and reciprocal relationship</u>." (SMM)*

# Chapter Seven

## Commit yourself and family to live for the sake of others.

**Our family pledges, through living for the sake of others, to perfect the world based on the culture of heart, which is rooted in the original lineage, by centering on true love.**

*Pledge number seven of the Family Pledge is important, although it is simple. The phrases, "Our family... rooted in the original lineage... centering on true love" are talking about inheriting the original lineage of Adam who does not have fallen lineage, which has nothing to do with the Fall. Then, it continues, "Our family...pledges to perfect the world based on the culture of heart, which is rooted in the original lineage..." Our world is to be a world based on the culture of heart. We are to be the Unification Family, one family, centered on the unique love of God. Without being high and low, all five races are to live as one family. Such a time is coming in the future. (SMM)*

### *The Original Lineage*

It is the original lineage centered on God. If we inherit this original lineage, the original culture of heart arises. Where the original lineage is lost, the culture of heart does not emerge. Culture is linked through history. The culture of heart should be a network of the family, society, nation, and world. "Our family...pledges to perfect the world based on the culture of heart, which is rooted in the original lineage..." This means that the issue is how to leave a pure lineage behind. Otherwise, our world based on the culture of heart is not realized.

Unless the world based on the culture of heart is established, the immense Kingdom of Heaven, where we are to live with the prepared foundation of heart, is cut off. For this reason, we should live a life based on the realm of the culture of heart.

The original lineage is no longer a fallen lineage. It is a lineage that has severed itself from Satan's lineage and restored the Fall through indemnity. It is the result of engrafting. When pulled out from the fallen root and engrafted to the true root, the third generation will receive the seeds of the original lineage.

The seeds from the engrafted tree should become original true olive trees. For this, three generations have to pass. This is serious. We need to approach this with confidence and determination. We are wild olive trees. Wild olive trees need to be engrafted to the true root as we cannot go back and be born again from our mother's womb. Then, after going through three generations, our offspring should come out as true olive trees. Three generations must pass for the cleansing to be complete.

This is accomplished by being blessed in marriage by Christ at his second coming, hence the name True Parents. That is why we talk about the Blessed Families being the foundation for the coming Kingdom of Heaven. We are actively participating with Christ in the building of it! Rev

Moon set about blessing as many couples as he could during His lifetime from all races and nations so that all of humanity could eventually participate. This tradition was passed on to His anointed heir and successor, Hyung Jin Moon, and will continue on into the future through that lineage. We are truly blessed to be alive at this time in history being able to actively participate in building God's Kingdom and bring God's lineage on to the earth for the first time.

I know that there will be some people who have a hard time with that concept, but think back to the time that Jesus walked on the earth. When you read the four gospels it is very obvious that all He wanted was to preach the gospel of the Kingdom and bring it to reality. Who were the ones who believed in him and supported His ministry? They were the salt of the earth, simple good hearted people and fishermen. The inteligencia of that time rejected Him. Will it be any different at His second coming? As this pledge says, it is based on the culture of heart, centering on God's true love.

### *Living for the sake of others*

Number seven of the Family Pledge says, "...to perfect the world based on the culture of heart, which is rooted in the original lineage..." There is something to be added: "through living for the sake of others." Through living for the sake of others, we are to perfect the world based on the culture of heart, which is rooted in the original lineage..." We need to add the phrase "through living for the sake of others." Living for the sake of others alone could be vague. So, we are to perfect the world based on the culture of heart through our concrete daily life – individual life, family life, and life in the larger society. Living for the sake of others is a concept as old as the bible, but as a way of life is something that has not happened except with a few notable exceptions. Even good people tend to put their family first and in today's secular society, how many times have you heard "you've got to take care of number one!"

"Through living for the sake of others... rooted in the original lineage, by centering on true love." It is love that serves. We should be able to feel love. It is something holy. We should be able to govern love. We should not do things as we please. We build a world based on the culture of heart through living for the sake of others. What is the world based on the culture of heart? It is the world based on the culture of God's love; we are pursuing the original world culture. It is the world of culture where there is no love to which true love is not related.

So when we base our life on true love, we automatically want to do everything for the sake of others. It used to be the common thing for a store clerk to ask the customer "how may I help you?" when we walked into a shop and may still be in some places. It makes you feel good doesn't it? Let's just make that our standard response to all we meet. And then act on it.

I know that many of us think that we do not want to be under the dominion of anyone else, no matter what. However, until now, we have not been able to fathom even in our dreams how happy it is to live under the dominion of the one who exists for the sake of others. Looking into the structure of the spirit world, God, the great Master of heaven and earth, is the center of all beings in the whole universe that exists for the sake of others. For this reason, it would be a great happiness to be governed by Him, but we have not understood how happy this would be. God had to establish the principle of living for the sake of others because He knows that it is here that the ideal realm of unification, where people can be grateful, is established for eternity.

Be a person who lives for the sake of others. This is the basis of the whole creation. God is this way and we are made to be in His image.

The next question is can we do this just by ourselves? Love is not realized when we are alone, so where does love come from? It does not come from us but from our relationships with others. Because it comes from these relationships, we must be ready to bow our head and serve others. This is where the heavenly principle, "live for the sake of others," comes from. When something extremely precious comes to us, we should exalt and serve others in order to receive it. We can receive love only when we have realized the philosophy of living for the sake of others. Even though you may think that this is very sacrificial, the benefits are extraordinary.

I think that we all want to be recognized, appreciated and loved. In today's fallen society a lot of people become famous for stupid things, but are forgotten a few years later or even sooner. The people that are revered and remembered with the most affection are those that have lived for the sake of others.

Living for the sake of others is also the starting point for world peace. The viewpoint of the principle of living for the sake of others, the noblest view of life, enables us to be happy while existing for the sake of all of humankind, existing for the sake of the whole world, existing for the sake of our nation, our society, our family, our spouse, and our children. There is no higher view of life than this.

It is critical that we perfect the world based on the culture of heart here in the physical world. In Mathew 16:19 Jesus said "whatsoever thou shalt bind on earth shall be bound in heaven: and whatsoever thou shalt loose on earth shall be loosed in heaven."

Habits last eternally in spirit world. This makes it very difficult to remove old habits once we pass away. However, this can be corrected on earth. If we develop stronger habits than our old habits, we can overcome them on earth. We must do it right now. Otherwise, we will be in trouble when we get to the spirit world.

The coming future world is the world of the new culture of heart and the culture of love based on the true family, where God, human beings, and all things live in harmony. It is the world of interdependence, mutual prosperity, and universally shared values in which people live for the sake of others in true love and live together in harmony and cooperation. The future history is to be one that realizes the dream of "humanity as brothers and sisters," transcending races with true love.

We should live with fun and joy in true love. We should be able to communicate with animals, harmonize with all things, and harmonize with God. Then there will be no such things as national boundaries. There will be no different cultures. It will be the culture of love. Since the culture of love is the culture of hobbies and recreational activities, a life of pursuing hobbies is love. Loving your spouse and loving your sons and daughters can be extended throughout the scope of the world. All are the expansion of your family and the realm of your object partners, celebrating culture. That is why the world based on the culture of heart where we enjoy ourselves is the culture of the Kingdom of Heaven on earth. It is the culture of hobbies and recreation. Such a culture of hobbies is the original culture of love, unrelated to the Fall. The culture of hobbies and recreation is the culture of the Kingdom of Heaven on earth.

In other words, we are pledging here to live for the sake of others, expressing God's love and bringing God's lineage to a reality here on earth first and then to the spiritual world when we pass over.

## Gaia's Gems for Personal Expansion

Gaia's Gem 7 - Heavenly Kingdom families

*"What do we have to love in order to love our nation?*
*First, a man should love a woman by regarding her as a representative of all women of this nation. Likewise, the woman, rather than thinking of the man as just one among many, should think of him as a representative of all the men in the entire world.*
*When a man and a woman regard each other as a representatives in this way and then unite and form a family,*
*this family will be a family of the heavenly Kingdom."*
(S.M.M.)

# Chapter Eight

## Commit yourself and family to the Kingdom of God on earth and in heaven.

**Our family, pledges, having entered the Completed Testament Age, to achieve the ideal of God and human beings united in love through absolute faith, absolute love and absolute obedience, and to perfect the realm of liberation and complete freedom in the Kingdom of God on earth and in heaven, by centering on true love.**

*But seek ye first the kingdom of God, and his righteousness; and all these things shall be added unto you. (Matt 6:33)*

### Completed Testament Age

The Completed Testament Age refers to a new age that begins now. It refers to the time when we can establish one unified world of peace through the oneness of families, tribes, peoples, nations and the world. This represents everyone, not only the family. By uniting the world, and uniting the whole universe, we enter the Completed Testament Age. When we establish a world that befits the Completed Testament Age, after uniting the present world through the new families based on the four realms of heart and the three kingships, we will finally have one world of peace.

It may not seem that way when we look around and see so much evil in the world but these are the last days predicted in Revelations by John. It is the time of tribulation. Evil is being exposed and Christianity is being persecuted as the battle rages (Rev 13: 6-8).It is time for the faithful to stand strong and pure (Rev 14:1-5) and hang on to Christ with our whole being, maintaining the vision of His Kingdom coming on earth as it is in Heaven.

So what is the Completed Testament Age? It is the time for uniting with, serving and caring for the True Parent (the Lord at His Second Advent) and Heavenly Father. We are moving into the period when human beings fulfill the 3 blessings given to us by God in Genesis and can act on behalf of God's authority, representing Him as His sons and daughters. An age full of hope is coming and we should quickly prepare for this before it is too late.

What promise is being fulfilled in the Completed Testament Age? It is the promise that God made to human beings at the time of creation when He gave man the 3 blessings (Gen 1:28). It is not the age of the providence of restoration (the Old Testament age) or the age of the providence of salvation (the New Testament age), but is the world of the ideal of creation that is to be realized. We are entering the age of the great transformation or change throughout the world.

The Completed Testament Age represents the fulfillment of God's covenant; that is, He is giving the Blessing to humankind. In the Old Testament Age, the Blessing did not occur; in the New Testament Age, the Blessing was desired; and in the Completed Testament Age, the Blessing is attained.

Is it not God's ideal of creation that Adam and Eve marry centering on God, thereby connecting the life force centered on His love to the life of Adam and Eve and leaving His lineage behind? Had this happened at the beginning, Adam and Eve would have become the True Parents. Now is the time for the restored Adam and Eve. True love is indeed great! Heavenly Father never gave up on us!

Things were offered in the Old Testament Age, sons and daughters in the New Testament Age, couples in the Completed Testament Age. And then you attend Heavenly Father.

As a result of the Fall, we human beings failed to attend God on earth, serving Satan instead and being separated from our Heavenly Father. We should now attend God and reconnect everything to Him.

It is ultimately to attend God on this earth that the Lord at his Second Advent, the True Parent, comes and suffers on this earth. Now we are in hell because all of humankind has been in service to Satan on earth. But the True Parent was victorious and by connecting to Him we can attend God through the application of true love.

It was to make this one road that the providence has been going through six thousand years of biblical history until now. Jesus tried to connect the New Testament Age to the Completed Testament Age and bring heaven and earth into oneness. He spent His ministry focusing on preaching the Kingdom. This, however, failed, due to the inability of the religious leaders of the day to unite with Him, and God's providence was prolonged for another two thousand years. Jesus brought spiritual salvation in the New Testament Age and worked to expand His scope to the world. The expansion movement produced many martyrs. Especially during the four hundred years of Roman persecution, many of his followers shed much blood. However, through that indemnity condition, the movement was expanded to the global level. Through this prolongation, God extended His providence of salvation to the world, hoping that the failures at the time of Jesus would be indemnified on the world level. Then, how could God's providence go beyond the New Testament Age and enter the Completed Testament Age? The Completed Testament Age refers to the realm of oneness of God and human beings. It refers to establishing, through true love, the realm of oneness, and standing on an equal basis by connecting together.

In this age we do not live with Satan but with God. Hence, the fallen realm must be eliminated. The elimination of Satan's world is possible because now is the time when all nations and the world can return to God. By clearly knowing about the details of the Kingdom of Heaven, we can eliminate the false world which goes against the principles of God.


## *Absolute faith, Absolute love and Absolute obedience*

In the Garden of Eden, Heavenly Father created with absolute faith, absolute love and absolute obedience. In other words, He completely invested Himself. The realm where Heavenly Father and human beings become one in love is therefore created through absolute faith, absolute love and absolute obedience (we completely invest ourselves). The Kingdom of Heaven on earth and in heaven is to be the realm of oneness of Heavenly Father and human beings in love, so that we, as His sons and daughters, who, like the absolute God, can freely exercise our full authority and responsibility. We can finally liberate God only when we become people of ability who can live this way

Everything was shattered due to lack of faith. This happened because Adam and Eve, the first human ancestors, failed to absolutely love God. They fell because of their inability to absolutely love and obey God. For this reason, the True Parents have indemnified this and prepared the highway for all of us to follow. Thus, if you practice absolute faith, absolute love and absolute obedience towards the True Parents, heaven and earth will respond and obey you, even if you call upon them day or night, and wake them up ten times. You should, therefore, not complain even if you are woken up a hundred times during the night. This is obedience.

Consensual obedience has within it a part of "self", but in absolute obedience this does not exist. You should be obedient even if it means following a thousand times a day.
The philosophy of the True Parents is simple. It is centered on absolute faith, absolute love and absolute obedience.
It is absolute faith centered on love. The absolute faith, however, is a concept, whereas love is the center of everything. Love is invisible although you experience it.

Next, obedience means practice. If we are going to realize love, centering on love, we must obey. The purpose of obedience is to achieve something greater; so, to achieve this we should invest ourselves without a thought of ourselves. If we try to follow centering on ourselves, it cannot fully grow. If we just view it from our own perspective we are following the way of the fall.

Americans, being individualists, are saying, "I am free! Why do I have to obey anybody?" When we talk about absolute faith, absolute love and absolute obedience, they say, "What kind of words are these? These are the words of a dictator or tyrant!" The communist thinking that "religion is the opiate of the elite" comes from the same background. This is Satan's philosophy as Satan also wants absolute obedience to himself. But Satan is not based on absolute love. This is the profound difference.

God created heaven and earth with absolute faith and absolute love, and in the position of absolute obedience. God's ideal of creation should therefore possess the same standards of absolute faith, absolute love and absolute obedience. Adam and Eve were the central beings; God's object partners of love. Thus, because creation was created with absolute faith, absolute love and absolute obedience, these become the standards for existence.

Christianity teaches faith, hope, and love. What is the greatest among them all? It is love. It is exactly the same. God created all things with absolute faith and absolute love. Absolute obedience requires you to have no sense of self; it requires that you be fully conscious of others. Hope does not refer to the present time; instead it is referring to the future expectations connected to the object partner. Hope is the same for both.

Absolute faith stands on the basis of absolute love, and absolute obedience stands on the basis of absolute love.

### *How is the oneness of God and humankind realized?*

Where does God's love and humankind's love meet? Where is their settlement point? That point becomes the settlement point of love, the settlement point of life, and the settlement point of lineage. Separated from that place, there would be no way of connecting love, life, and lineage. Where on earth is that place? It is where the lives of a man and a woman are connected. It is where the lineage, the blood of a man and a woman, cross. God's life, God's love, God's lineage, and the life of a man and a woman, the love of a man and a woman, and the lineage of a man and a woman, are connected at this one point. And their descendants arise at this point.

Adam and Eve having their children of goodness, and becoming the true parents, means that God physically secures His position as the eternal Parent, and realizes His ideal and desire to have an endless number of citizens of the Kingdom of Heaven in heaven and on earth through their multiplication from generation to generation.

God created Adam first as His body. Adam is God's son, and at the same time God Himself with a body as well. Next, God created Eve as Adam's partner in an effort to perfect the horizontal love, that is, the ideal of conjugal love. Eve is God's daughter and, at the same time, His bride who is to physically perfect God's ideal of horizontal love. The place where Adam and Eve have reached perfection, and consummate their first love after marriage under God's blessing, is also the place where God receives His physical bride. God's ideal of absolute love vertically comes down to, and participates in, where Adam and Eve's ideal of conjugal love horizontally bears fruit. God's true love and humankind's true love start at one point, centering on the starting point of the vertical and horizontal, bear fruit, and reach perfection.

When we realize that this is God's ideal we can see that the blessing in marriage between one man and one woman is the goal of creation. Any other "marriage" relationship is the direct result of the fall, and therefore has nothing to do with God but with Satan.

In the world of atoms, electrons revolve around the protons. In the world of molecules, the plus ions and minus ions interact. Those that interact do so with a center. Man and woman also interact. Centering on what? They interact centering on love. God and human beings also interact. What does the phrase, "oneness of God and humankind", mean? We also use the term "union". Centering on what, is oneness achieved? Centering on what, do we talk about the oneness of parents and children and the oneness of husband and wife? It is centering on love. The parents and children, and the husband and wife, are united as one body. This is the oneness of God and humankind. Centering on what? Centering on money, on political power, or on knowledge? It is beyond doubt that it is centering on love. What kind of love is it? It is true love, and Godly love. What kind of love is Godly love? It is absolute love. What is absolute love? It is aligned with eternity. It is eternal love.

Had Heavenly Father established the desired relationship of true love with human beings, and thus built the ideal family embodying the oneness of Heavenly Father and humankind, today we would all be in the Kingdom of Heaven and hell would not exist. The problem here is that unless God and human beings become one in true love as subject-object partners, and make a start at the same one point, the true love of God and the love of humankind will have different directions and purposes; their loves starting in two different forms. Then, it would be impossible to find the absolute world of the ideal desired by God and human beings. This is the unfortunate and cataclysmic situation we have seen in the world throughout history. Adam and Eve did not center themselves on God and His love but on Satan.

The Fall of Adam and Eve is the immoral sin that forsook God's ideal of true love. Adam and Eve, before the Fall, needed to keep the commandment, but fell at the stage of immaturity during the growth period.

The union of the first love of the human ancestors, since being the perfection of God's love as well at the same time, should surely have been a continuation of happy feasts in which God, Adam and Eve, and all things naturally became intoxicated in joy and blessings. It should have been a happy ceremony in which God's love, life, and lineage formed a beginning and settled in human beings. However, they, instead, covered their lower parts and hid behind the tree, trembling in fear. This is because they, in violation of the heavenly path, perpetrated the immoral relationship that gave rise to the source of false love, false life, and false lineage.

Satan entered where God should have. Adam and Eve and Satan married, didn't they? It is the same thing. If Adam and Eve had not fallen, God's true love and humankind's love would have united at one point. They were to start at one point; if it were two points, there would be two different worlds and two different directions. Yet, if they achieved the oneness of God and humankind, and went in one direction, the individuals who appear in one direction would reach perfection; the family that appears in one direction would reach perfection; and also the tribe, people, nation and world that appear in the one direction would reach perfection. They would become one in love. This would agree with the theory.

What is the difference between the established Christian churches and this teaching? One difference is that this teaching restores the oneness of God and humankind centering on love. Established theologies define God as holy, and human beings as profane and sinful. Then, how can God's love and humankind's love become one? They cannot answer this question. The problem is that they think the absolute God can do anything. This was the main reason why Christians shed so much blood wherever they went. Misusing God's commandment, they invaded and seized. They produced dictators. The original world, however, should not work like that. From the viewpoint of God's original nature, it cannot be like that.

## *The realm of liberation and complete freedom in the Kingdom of God on earth and in heaven*

If Adam and Eve had not fallen, what would God have wanted to give them? God wanted to bless and marry them, have them give birth to sons and daughters in whom He could rejoice, and form God's family in whom He could rejoice, and form His tribe and His people, by multiplying. When they expanded further and formed the world, what philosophy would they be based on? It would be the world of Godism and the Adam centered philosophy. If that world had a philosophy, it would be the philosophy centered on Adam. If that world had a view of the universe, it would be Adam's view of the universe, an Adam-centered philosophy. If it had a view of the cosmos, it would be Adam's view of the cosmos; and if it had a view of life, it would be Adam's view of life based on that Adam-centered philosophy. And when the five different races had various colors of skin, it would not matter. Skin colors changed according to the environment and countless people having different skin colors is okay. Then, why did the languages of the countless peoples differ? God separated them, due to the Fall of the first human ancestors.

When it comes to a nation, establishing a nation requires sovereignty. It requires a people. It requires land. When considering the question of establishing the Kingdom of Heaven on earth from this point of view, who is the owner of the Kingdom of Heaven? Who is the sovereign? Surely, God is the sovereign, represented by Christ, the King of Kings. And who are the citizens? It is humankind. Then, what is the territory? It is the planet earth. This is the long awaited culmination of the End of Time as prophesied in Biblical scriptures and is the true realm of liberation and complete freedom. This will be a real physical Kingdom. What are countries now will be states just as in the United States of America, but this Kingdom will be like no other that has previously existed.

As a sovereign nation it will require a constitution. In the preamble to the *Constitution of the United States of Cheon Il Guk* (Kingdom of Heaven) it states:

"This Establishment of the Kingship of God, marks the end of Satan's Kingships of past tyranny and domination over the peoples of this world throughout time. By the Complete Victory of the True Father, Sun Myung Moon – King of Kings and Lord of Lords, the conditions were met to establish God's Physical Kingdom on this Earth. However, due to the failure of Han Mother at the final hour, the world moves through a period of judgment instead of blessing and the providence has been extended over three generations through the Three Kingships of God.

In the beginning of human history in the Garden of Eden, God's original world of freedom, liberty, conscience, and relationship with God was to be established. It was to be a world where the powerful archangels were to be the servants of the children of God. However, due to the Fall, Eve committed adultery with the Archangel and tempted Adam into sinning against God. Thus, the world of Satan's domination over mankind was established and history has shown centralized powers, either governmental, religious or financial, use artificial structures and power to rule over mankind sometimes taking freedoms gradually and sometimes eliminating them by brute force. God's Kingdom on Earth must be established where the artificial structures of power, representing Satan, shall never again rule over mankind and humanity. The Role of the Kingships of God, must be to preserve and protect this covenant between God and the peoples of this world."

We are living in the most amazing time of all history – the birth of the Kingdom of God on earth! Savor it, participate in the building of it, and bring true happiness to God and all of mankind! *Amen and Hallelujah*!

# Gaia's Gems for Personal Expansion

## Gaia's Gem 8 - COMMUNICATION

*I commit to communicate clearly about my emotions and let others be free to express themselves, as I will listen with the intent to understand them.*

 I'll take courage to stretch myself beyond my limitations and speak of what I notice even if difficult to say it, when someone speaks or act from a scatter part of his or her personality.. I go to my body to find the truth. I'll take responsibility for my feelings, my actions, of what I'm experiencing.
Is what I'm communicating closely expressing what I'm actually experiencing? Can I hear the clear intentional wanting in others communication?

# Acknowledgements and Thank you

I would like to acknowledge and appreciate my wife Gaia for not only the initial inspiration to write this book, but also for her continual encouragement and support. She was always there when I needed, and guided me to include the more personal anecdotes.

I would especially like to thank Reverend Sun Myung Moon whose words I studied to get the full meaning of this content, and his son and heir Hyung Jin Moon for his incredible insights into the world today.

I would like to thank Kristen Joy and the Kindle in 30 challenge for helping me to get this book written and published.

Thank you for taking the time read this book. We trust that you have received inspiration and hope from it. Please pass it on to all those you care about and leave a review on Amazon

# About the authors

Rob Carvell, born in England, came to the USA in 1976, this country's bicentennial. He spent the next 12 years on the spiritual frontlines working with various programs and crusades, eventually becoming a pastor in Austin TX and then Little Rock AR.
In 1988 he moved to NY to build a TV and recording studio complex for the church and stayed on to help in its operations for 28 years.

Gaia Carvell, born in Italy, came to America in 1986. She focused on raising and caring for her children, but was always ready to share her faith where ever, and with whoever she could. In 2015, after serving for a number of years with an Anglican Bishop in a senior facility, she received an MA as a Chaplain.

They now live in NE Pennsylvania and are both active in the World Peace and Unification Sanctuary simply known as Sanctuary Church.

Made in the USA
Lexington, KY
07 February 2018